Silhouette Soldiers
& Other Verse

Ted Morgan

First published in the UK in 2019
Violet Circle Publishing.

Manchester, England, UK.
ISBN: 978-1-910299-19-7

Text Copyright © Ted Morgan 2019.

Cover Design Copyright © VCP 2019

All rights are reserved: no part of this may be stored in a retrieval system, reproduced or transmitted by any means, electronic, mechanical, photocopying, or otherwise without the prior written permission of the publisher, in accordance with the terms of licenses issued by the Copyright Licensing Agency.

All characters and scenarios in this publication are fictitious and any resemblance to real persons, living or dead is purely coincidental.

British Library Cataloguing in Publication Data.
A catalogue record for this book is available from the British Library.

All papers used in the production of this book are sourced only from wood grown in sustainable forests.

www.violetcirclepublishing.co.uk

For,

*Robin and Corinne,
With thanks for all your help
and encouragement.*

Contents

Silhouette Soldiers 1
Britain Alone 2
Manchester Hill 3
A Childhood War 5
D -Day 7
One Hundred Years 9
Aging Valentine 10
Alison and The Spider 11
An Autumnal Ode 12
Ann Margaret Redburn R.I.P. 13
Bonfire Night 14
Computer Fit 16
Christmas Day Remembrance 17
Domesticity 18
Crackers !! 19
Christmas Poem 2016 21
Four Years 22
Cricket Confusion 23
Christmas Poem 2017 25
Duvet Day 27
Life Advice 28
Christmas Floods 29

Going to IKEA 31

Halloween Night 33
Hope 34
Christmas poem 2018 35

Inertia 36

Kearsley Power Station 37

Iron Man *38*
Loneliness *39*
Languidity *40*
The Spirit of Christmas *41*
Mum's Washday *43*
My Manchester *45*
The North and the South *46*
The Robin *47*
The Spider *48*
The Room *49*
The Yule Log *51*
Thoughts on a farewell *52*
Washing Mishap *53*
Winter Days *54*
Witches Party *55*
My walking mats *56*
Nativity *57*
On Camera *59*
Parliamentary Politics *60*
Post Festive Thoughts *61*
Potholes *62*
Rambling *63*
The Trip *65*
The Ache Inside *68*
The Blackbird *69*
The Church *70*
Moonbeams *71*

When I look back, I realise now the big impact that the Great War had on my life even though I was born 20 years after its conclusion in 1938. My Father fought in the battle of Manchester Hill and was shot in the head, taken prisoner and tended by the Germans. He was repatriated in 1919 to a hospital in Edinburgh. After he was demobilised, he suffered from the effects of that conflict until his death, the day after my 9th birthday in 1947. My mother always said that the man who came back from the conflict was not the same man who enlisted in 1916.

I have written many poems about my childhood during the 39/45 war, my dad was on low wages, food was scarce and we were poor, most people on our Manchester Council estate were in the same situation. I grew up without the influence of a father in my teenage years, my mother had to go to work and I became a "latch key kid." The key hung round my neck and down my shirt. Money was always tight and if I wanted anything I either made it myself or did without.

I think quite a few of the many poems I have written

reflect this, both in this book and in my other published works.

Two things helped me during this period .One was the local library and the other was the Boy Scout Movement, they provided me with an insight into other people's lives, and also introduced me to the country side pursuits of rambling, climbing and pot holing ,I have a love of the open moorland that has stayed with me, I was a member of a mountain Rescue team for over 20 years.

I served in the Royal Air Force as a medic and when demobbed qualified as a registered general and psychiatric nurse, rising to a senior nurse administrative position before my retirement.

I have seen the best and at times the worse in the human condition, and some of my poems reflect this, though I must admit that this is at times tempered by my warped sense of humour.

I hope that you enjoy this volume.

Silhouette Soldiers

These images appeared one day on lawns and public spaces,
They gathered round like phantoms from the past to celebrate,
The hundred years since the armistice of the great war,
Silent black figures, a stark reminder of the men who fought and died,
And also, the many thousands whose lives were blighted by that conflict,
The widows bringing up children whose fathers had paid the ultimate price,
Or men whose mental torment caused by that horrific conflict,
Changed them for ever, they were not the smiling men who enlisted,
The "land fit for hero's " promise was never kept;
No jobs and poverty were the recompense for their sacrifice,
And a few years later, war again caused turmoil in Europe,
If nothing else these silhouettes remind us all of the futility of war.

Britain Alone

It was in the nineteen fortys,
That Britain stood alone,
The little ships at Dunkirk,
Had rescued our army from the Hun,
And high above our island,
Defending Britain's sky's,
The Spitfires and the Hurricanes,
Battled Germans might,
Bombers came each evening,
And fire raged in London Town,
But the gallant British people,
Endured this fiery hell each night,
Their spirit was not broken,
As they continued in the fight,
German losses were so great,
The sky's they couldn't control,
So the invasion that they had planned,
Had to be put on hold,
The Spitfires and the Hurricane's,
Flown by Churchills gallant "few,"
Had won the battle of the skies,
But many brave pilots we lost too,
Four more years had passed,
Before we set foot on Frances shores again,
And along with our allies'
A victory we could claim.

My father fought and was wounded and captured by the Germans in this Battle, which was fought on the 21st March 1918.

Manchester Hill

The 16th Manchester's gathered round,
Whilst Colonel Elstob told the plan,
To defend the small and grassy hill,
And hold it to a man,
"Here we fight and here we die,"
Was the rallying cry they heard,
Whilst the German guns began to roar,
Our men, resolute not deterred.

A swirling mist obscured the field,
Of the gunners' line of fire,
And the German troops like phantoms,
Moved in mud and stranded wire,
Attackers charged wave on wave,
But the lads showed firm resolve,
And beat back the Hun invaders,
In the battle that evolved.

The Manchester's killed and wounded,
Littered trenches all around,
But they still held on to that grassy knoll,
They were ordered to defend,
They had stemmed the flow of the Hun advance,
And gave the British time,
To strengthen the defences,
Of the long rear battle line.

At 4pm their race was run,
Their colonel dead and gone,
Midst other men from Manchester,

Who joined deaths echelon,
Seventy-six who fell that day,
Caused tears at home to flow,
The wounded and the captured,
Dealt a heartfelt savage blow.

But pride in their achievement,
At holding out so long,
Ensured a lasting memory that remains forever strong,
Northern grit had triumphed,
On that field in far flung France,
And should never be forgotten,
As the years continue to advance.

I was a young lad during the 1939-1945 war and this was how it was.

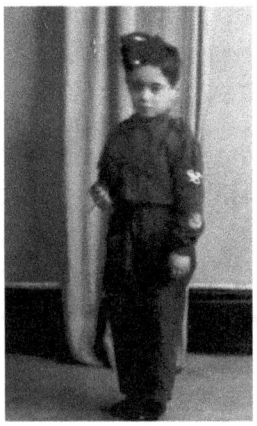

A Childhood War

When I was a lad I went to school,
With wellies for shoes which was against the rule,
But how could I say all the money was spent,
On food for the table, and to pay the rent,
My dad he died early, as a result of the Great War,
And my mum she straggled just to feed us all.

I had two sisters much older than me,
And I was the "baby" as was plain to see,
It was in war time which was a great blow,
My sister's they worked, but wages were low,
One packed parachute for the men at the front,
The other made macs with needles,
She said that were blunt.

At school we had milk, in a bottle so small,
And dinners were bad, just stogie mash that was all,
The Germans came over and bombed our fair city,

Many buildings they crashed, which was a great pity,
In school, we behaved or else got the strap,
And believe me when I tell you it wasn't just a tap.

Few sweets in the shop, only 2 ounces a week,
With rations and coupons no room for food pique,
You ate what was put there, no fads were allowed,
You had tripe, and trotters, and brawn from pig's jowls.

Few presents at Christmas no turkey or goose,
A rabbit maybe, washed down with some juice,
Pennies in't gas meter, no washers or phone
Just wireless for news, most women alone,
Their men at the front fighting the foe,
When the call came, men just had to go.

Washdays were Mondays, with wringer and tub,
In winter its drying, in the house caused a fugg,
Socks they were darned, not thrown out like now,
Clothes patched when holes came,
But we managed somehow.

Men they came home from places far flung,
To girlfriends and wives, parted by war for too long,
And a nation remembered the people they lost,
And many families counted their own grievous loss.

In tribute to the men who fought and died on the Normandy Beaches.

D -Day

At one time Britain stood alone,
Against the Fuhrer's might,
Then allies joined them in their quest,
To help Britain win its fight,
They planned a big invasion,
To take back what had been lost,
With many thousand troops amassed,
And a Channel to be crossed.

Boats and sea borne forces,
Stood expectant for D- Day,
Waiting for the orders,
To set them on their way,
So many men had planned for this,
Success was not assured,
And for the youthful warriors massed,
The waiting they endured.

Most lads were only 18 or 20 at the most,
Called up to join the forces,
They truly had no choice,
Operation Overlord, was the name it had been given,
To boot the Germans out of France,
Was their deadly mission.

Beaches out in Normandy,
Had all been given names,
Juno, Sword and Omaha,
Were soon to be proclaimed.

The Para troops they went in first,
At H Hour they did drop,
Securing guns and bridges,
So re-enforcements they could stop,
The seaborne troops then landed,
On beaches swept with fire,
The strong resistance left the bodies,
Draped over the beaches wire.

Young lads grew into men that day,
Heroic deeds abound,
But many men were killed,
With mayhem all around,
The sights and sound of battle,
Continued through the day,
But slowly they advanced through hell,
But there was a price to pay.

A bridgehead was established,
And supplies though it were poured,
To continue helping the assault to beat the Nazi hoard,
Tanks and lorries rumbled,
Through the lanes of Norman France,
And patriotic French citizens,
Hailed our forces brave advance.

The beachhead was expanded,
Our foothold made secure,
And soldiers, sailors, airmen had many battles to endure,
And after many months of conflict,
Victory it was won,
And Europe it was free from the jackboot of the Hun.

Though many years have passed since that fateful day,
We still enjoy the freedoms,
Bought with hero's blood today.

Written to celebrate the anniversary of the end of the first world war.

One Hundred Years

It's a hundred years since the silence fell,
Where mud had created a living hell,
So many died in this four-year war,
As bullets and guns stopped their senseless roar.

Men emerged from entombed trenches and lines,
Where they had lived within claustrophobic confines,
And bells rang out proclaiming peace,
When the noise of the battle at last did cease,
But what of the men who'd been killed or maimed,
The mentally damaged by this battle insane.

No glory or kudos by their medals displayed,
The soldiers they knew the price that they'd paid,
And families back home breathed a great sigh,
And celebrated the return of their beloved alumni,
But the war to end wars was just a dream,
For since then war has been a recurrent theme.

Aging Valentine

I am an aging Valentine,
My waist no longer trim,
My eyesight is not so sharp,
My hearing rather grim,
I can't even cut my toenails,
My skin is dry and scaly,
I've lots of moles and pimples too,
But I wash my tootsies daily.

My joints seem rather creaky,
I don't kneel upon my knees,
So as you see, on this lover's day,
Romance is just a tease,
So, I will just raise a glass,
And toast you all with hearty cheers,
And wish you all a romance,
That will last throughout the years.

This happened!!

Alison and The Spider

Alison sits there crocheting completely unaware,
That above her was a spider eyeing up her hair,
He thought, in that tangle I could make a mighty web,
He then proceeded downwards,
Towards her unprotected head.

As the creature abseiled downwards,
Thinking this will be a breeze,
Its sighting in a mirror, caused Alison to freeze,
Her mouth it opened slightly,
She gave a blood curdling scream,
Then rushed towards the doorway,
Scared stiff in the extreme.

Both daughters they looked up,
And laughed at mums hysterical display,
"Its only a small spider mum"
Was all that they could say,
The spider it scurried off, its plans now truly thwarted,
Whilst Alison now more composed,
Her anguish now aborted.

An Autumnal Ode

We walk beneath the myriad colours,
Of autumnal rainbow leaves,
Each tree bedecked in bridal gowns,
Of greens and reds and gold,
The sun is high in cloudless sky,
But an autumnal chill is felt,
Whilst squirrels dart from tree to tree,
To gather nuts to hoard,
Some birds fly south to warmer climes,
To escape the approaching cold,
Whilst others find deep hollows,
To sleep though winters hours,
Flowers last flush of the summer,
Are struck down by night time chills,
Autumn's icy blasts will cause the leaves to fly and fall,
And what is left are skeletal trees,
And mists that shroud them all.

My second book of poetry was dedicated to Ann, sadly she died of cancer on 3rd of October 2018.

Ann Margaret Redburn R.I.P.

She fell asleep last Wednesday,
My friend of 40 years,
Her voice no more will talk to me,
About her hopes and fears,
Her laughter no longer ripples,
And fills a room with joy,
Her smile a fleeting memory no longer to enjoy,
I walk the lanes of memories,
And recollect the times,
When we marvelled at the beauty,
Of autumnal nature's signs,
Or talked at length about a book,
Or verse that touched our soul,
So many things remembered,
Our sadness to console.

This was a commission from my grandchildren, as they love Bonfire Night.

Bonfire Night

The bonfire flames rise in the sky,
Rockets soar on high,
They burst into a myriad stars,
Their crackling fills the sky,
Whilst round the bonfire burning bright,
Are lots of eager faces,
Waiting for the spuds to cook,
So they can feed their faces,
Sparklers weave their magic light as,
Children twist and whirl,
Catherine wheels spin merrily,
As round a nail they twirl,
This cavalcade of sparking light,
With colours red and green,
On Bonfire Night it's as you know,
A country wide played scene.

Written after a conversation with one of my sons many years after my divorce.

Reflections on a Break Up.

A young boy came from school one day,
"Where's my dad?" He asked his mum,
She really did not want to say,
Just where his dad had gone,
Whilst young the marriage broke up,
Both parties were to blame,
But the truth is sometimes hidden,
With excuses that are lame,
The boy grew up without a dad,
To show him manly things,
Whilst single mums try very hard,
To bridge the gap it brings,
If parents only thought about,
The impact of their strife,
And how it can affect all,
And their children's later life,
Both parents need to compromise,
Allow access to their spouse,
So, balance can be maintained,
In their children's dwelling house,
Male and female guidance,
Shape how their children learn,
The rights and wrongs of living,
During the wheel of life's slow turn,
It is not always possible,
For this pattern to fit each child,
But try and make it happen,
Do not by rancour be beguiled.

Computer Fit

My computer will not just behave;
Its thrown a fit and made me rage,
Any orders typed it just ignores,
And happily searches without pause,
As if its searching for a mate,
A female gigabyte for a date.
I sit and stare in wonderment;
Praying for it to abate,
As my curser wanders near and far,
And ignores commands whilst I just stare,
My poor brain is in a whirl,
Its driving me to deep despair.
I cannot write, I cannot search,
The internet's left me in the lurch,
And e-mails appear to clog my box,
But their secrets I just can't unlock,
I've had a pill to calm my nerves,
But tranquil thoughts seem so perverse.
I want to smash this techno thing,
But if I do the tills will ring,
A Greek has taken my machine,
A Trojan horse is on the screen,
Though Troy is nowhere near my place,
Its navigations is a disgrace.
How can I get this darn thing shifted?
I need a geek that's pretty nifty,
I do know one who's intervention,
Makes motherboards pay attention,
Makes cursor obey commands,
With just a mouse in her hands,
My anguish then will pass away,
And a compliant computer will make my day.

Christmas Day Remembrance

This Christmas day a father and two brothers meet,
Many years since this last occurred,
So much has happened in our lives,
To shape the contours of our being,
But this day is special to each one of us,
A family though shattered by untold events,
May we all relive this day in future years,
For family is the heart of all our existence,
We will not always see eye to eye,
But respect and love lie deep within our soul,
Let us rejoice at this time and treasure its memory,

Domesticity

I am just a single aged bloke,
Domestic goddess I am not,
I just hate doing the ironing,
And cleaning up the grot.

My house is hardly spotless,
My piles of dust they glow,
And when the sunlight catches them,
I'm afraid they start to show.

My windows have a "live in" look,
With streaks; just one or two,
But in my defence, it must be said,
I have a spotless loo.

The oven I hate cleaning,
But if the door is shut, unseen,
The grill pan I protect with foil,
That's How I keep it clean.

I have a carpet that is brown,
So stains they do not show,
And subdued lighting in the room,
Make cobwebs vision low.

I keep the bedroom door shut tight,
For its my storage room,
With curtains closed all day,
You can't see what's in the gloom.

This is my special refuge,
From obsessive cleaning types,
They'd drive me nuts during the day,
And would have to work at night.

An ode in bad taste, due to my Psychiatric Nurse training and warped sense of humour.

Crackers !!

People said I was crackers,
That I was not right in the head,
So, to prove I was sane, and right in the head,
And my brain was not really screwed,
I made an appointment with a psychiatrist,
Which I'm afraid altered my mood.

With high trepidation and panic I went in,
And he said, "what's wrong?"
"I can see that this visit disturbs you,
Have you felt like this for long?"
"No doc" I said in a whisper,
"This visit has made me this way,"
"Your blaming me for your Paranoia,"
Was all that the doctor could say.

My heart started beating faster,
And round my head I felt a tight band,
My palms they were sweaty, as I started to panic,
And with my voice I made not a sound,
"Classic anxiety syndrome, "
Was the doctors next voiced remark,
"Overlaid with a complex inferior,
Urgent treatment should start."

"I'm right in the head" I shouted,
"It's you that has made me this way,
All this Psycho Hocus pokus,
Is causing my brain cells to stray."

"Ah! Early dementia has started,
I think that I'm right on the ball,
I'll now give you tests that will tell,
How much you can clearly recall."

At that I was off like a shot,
Through the door and down the street I did run,
Went into the first pub that I encountered,
And ordered a large double rum.

"You've been to see doc down the street,"
The landlord did say,
"Gives my business a heck of a boost.
He's as daft a brush, not normal at all,
but the Asylum's just let him loose."

Each year I write a Christmas verse which I usually put in my Christmas Cards.

Christmas Poem 2016

An old lady stood at a graveside,
Her face it was drawn and so sad,
Snow softly falling on the grave,
Where she'd buried her lad,
Her loss occurred at Christmas,
A season of faith and joy,
But a car ride on roads that were icy,
Was how she lost her dear boy,
So now at each Christmas that passes;
She finds a young lad all alone,
And gives him a meal and a present;
Inviting him into her home,
The gap in her life lasts for ever,
But this ritual she does every year,
Bringing memories of her boys' past yuletides,
Her actions bring one boy good cheer,
Her memories of Christmas are now filled,
With faces who shared her repast,
As she honours the memory of her loss,
With a kindness and trust that will last,
For the helping of others at yuletide,
Helps to dull the ache that she feels,
As she thinks of her own boy at Christmas,
And the good deed that helps her ache heal.

These lines were written on the fourth anniversary of my wife's death.

Four Years.

Four years have passed,
But time I feel has stood still,
The ache I felt so many months ago,
Has not yet diminished,
Memories fill my mind with scenes,
Of good and bad times,
Life still goes on,
But I sometimes feel as though it has stopped,
When a love was as strong as I felt,
It is impossible to let it go,
It encompasses your very being,
And fills your every waking hour,
My memories make life bearable,
Yet quietude and solitude,
Help make the present cope,
With the loss of the past.

Written to take the micky out of a cricket fanatic I know.

Cricket Confusion

In our village, on the green,
Plays our local cricket team,
A friend who's totally absorbed,
Showed me the "ropes" or so he thought,
But confusion reigned within my brain,
Of terms I think so very strange,
After explaining cricket for an hour,
My fact-soaked brain he's rearranged.

He took me out to the crease,
But no wrinkles did I see,
Showed me the stumps,
They all looked tall, not felled like yonder tree,
He said "that man's a bowler,"
But his hat he did not doff.

The batsman then took his stance,
And said "middle and off,"
I know he's is in the middle,
But why should he depart?
No one's bowled a ball at him,
The game to me should start.

That mans at silly point he said,
But even I could see,
It was a stupid place to stand,
Too near the bat was he,
He's got four slips my friend did say,
But skirt's they did not wear.

My gosh! he's bowled a "Yorker",
But no chocolate bar was there,
Then he bowled a "Googly",
That's a search engine for sure,
Bur no lurking laptops did I see,
On which to put a score.

There were two men in long white coats,
The umpires were their names,
They waved their arms about a lot;
At points within the game.

He said that mans the night watchman,
But a lamp he has not got,
But no one's going to pinch the pitch:
I think I've lost the plot.

I heard a shout of "no ball,"
But I'm sure I saw one thrown,
Then when a shout of "bye" was heard,
Do players all go home?

My head is Oh! so confused,
I think I'll take a nap,
Cricket has me snookered,
In a mid-off, leg-side trap!!

Christmas Poem 2017

The Christmas seasons on us,
With glitz in all the shops,
Tinsel, trees and baubles,
Winter scarves and fancy socks,
Christmas cards displayed,
Whilst carols fill the air,
The shopping pandemonium,
For gifts to show we care.

But does this splurge of excess,
Have any meaning for us all,
Or do we have to spend, spend, spend,
At every market stall,
Its meaning in this day and age,
Seems to have passed us by,
A big commercial enterprise is all we do espy.

What of the birth in Bethlehem?
When our saviour Christ was born,
No glitzy crib for him at all,
But a stable all forlorn,
Poor shepherds came to visit him,
Just curious to see,
The wonderous thing that happened,
That impacts you and me.

For Christmas is a time of joy,
For family and our friends,
To show how much we treasure them,
And sometimes to make amends.

Let us try and share our goods,
With folks whose life is hard,
For Christ had no earthly comforts,
In that cold stable yard.

The spirit that is Christmas shows,
To go that extra mile,
To help the old and lonely,
Share our joy just for a while.

Duvet Day

I lie in bed and hear the rain,
Thundering down outside,
As underneath the blankets I lie,
Snug and warm inside,
Within my head are lots of things,
That I should do today,
But listening to the falling rain,
It does not make my day.

There are so many things to do,
The dust needs moving round,
And the thought of all the ironing,
Make my heart just pound and pound,
And pots are piled up in the sink,
From last night's Sunday roast,
And scattered round the toaster,
Crumbs from yesterday's breakfasts toast.

My eyes are closed to outside light,
And thoughts whirl in my head,
But none of them, I am sure,
Involves my getting out of bed.

Today I'll have a Duvet day,
And dream though daylight hours,
Ignoring all the tasks I list,
As I take my morning shower,
But alas my bodily functions,
Thwarts these random rebellious muses,
For I must rise to use the loo and abandon my excuses.

Life Advice

Good mental health I am told,
Is impotant to us all,
How we cope in this modern life,
Amid its stress and its pitfalls,
We have to learn to cope with change and uncertainty,
And form some good relationships,
With the likes of you and me,
To maintain this equilibrium,
It is essential that we talk,
And verbalise our feelings,
To those most near and friends,
And not resort to alcohol when loneliness abounds,
Keep active and eat well is a mantra that should lead,
And keep us on our chosen path,
As wellbeing is achieved,
Don't trivialise your talents,
Accept your shortcomings with grace,
And you will live a contented, fruitful life,
With good mental healthh in place.

Written after the Christmas floods of 2018.

Christmas Floods

Noah he was up in heaven,
He thought he'd have a lark,
I'll drown them northern moorlands,
That'll do just for a start,
I'll have to get permission though,
From 'yed Mon' hereabouts,
I'll tell him folks bin naughty,
And deserve a great big clout,
They'll have to build some Arks like mine,
But not with plans from me,
Am afraid they'll have to scratch their heads,
And make their own you see.

But times have changed since Noah's day,
An' Northern folk are strong,
They don't build Arks any more,
For sheep and cattle "pong,"
It poured with rain in Lancashire,
And Yorkshire got a wetting,
And rivers overflowed their banks,
And folks they started fretting.

They battled for their houses,
So people pulled together,
And showed that northern spirit,
But prayed for fairer weather,
Northern grit will triumph,
And Noah's plan could well backfire,
When all backs are to the wall,
Their courage will inspire.

Volunteers they came from near and far,
To lend a helping hand,
To clean and sweep the houses,
In this wet and rain-soaked land,
Getting back to normal,
Will take many days to right,
But folk of Northern England,
Will not give up the fight.

Let's hope the powers in London,
Will plan to make them safe,
By the dredging of the rivers,
And put flood barriers in place,
So people in these northern lands,
Can sleep safely in their homes,
And not have go a wading,
When the local river decides to roam.

After my first visit to a very large Store near my home town I had to write this.

Going to IKEA

I've heard a lot about IKEA,
And the great goods that they sell,
But there is a big problem,
That to you I really must tell.

You enter in quite innocently,
And are sucked into its web,
Go up the escalator,
To the land of the living dead.

Bright lights and fluffy cushions,
Children's toys as well,
But it draws you like a magnet,
Into a nightmare living hell.

You don't know where you wander,
No exit in your sight,
For you begin to wonder,
If they let you out at night.

Round and round you wander,
Like water goes down plugs,
And in a daze you travel,
As though you're high on drugs.

Bedrooms, bathrooms, kitchens,
Assail your weary eyes,
You tramp around the store,
But the exits they disguise.

At last you find a helpful map,
Painted on a board,
But when you start to follow it,
You're back where you've just explored.

At last you find a staff member,
Who knows the store terrain,
She puts you on the right path,
And says nicely "come again,"
At last you see the checkout,
Where they relive you of your cash,
Your mind's still kind of hazy,
As to your car you dash!

Halloween Night

The ghosties and ghouls are all flying,
To celebrate Halloween this year,
Off to the dark dismal castle,
To feast on wine, blood and beer,
The vampires have had their teeth sharpened,
To bite any neck that's around,
Whilst Zombies gather and stand there,
On strike so they don't make a sound,
There very annoyed at the witches,
For a Union they've formed don't you know,
But Zombies cannot be members,
For flying on broomsticks to them is no go,
The Bats are out in their thousands,
Taking the dim dismal night air,
Enjoying the soft shadows of moonlight,
And giving the occasional scare,
Count Dracula he is the boss man,
Of the wizards and warlocks and crones,
And he's dining tonight in his castle,
On heart, sheep's liver and bones,
His goblet is filled to the brim,
With maid's blood and a whisper of gin,
So don't go out tonight,
Or your neck he will bite,
So you'll belong forever to him,
You now know why Halloween's scary,
Why indoors you must try to reside,
With a cross and a stake and some garlic,
For protection if you venture outside.

Hope

Its funny how when one feels low,
Your troubles seem to grow and grow,
All the wrongs that you have done,
Oppress and cling, blot out the sun,
Clouds hang low, and mist pervades,
Each mountain top and woodland glade,
We need that hope when we feel low,
To make our anguish flee and go,
To see a glimmer of a future bright,
Instead of downcast anguished nights,
Hold on to hope for better days,
Your persistence will not be betrayed,
Like all things, the feelings of despair,
Will vanish in the sunlit air,
Your countenance now bears a smile,
Your hopes not fear, will you beguile,
So, hang on to hope when you feel low,
To see a brighter future grow.

Christmas poem 2018

The Armistice was signed in Nineteen eighteen,
And the Christmas that followed was joyfully seen,
As a time for rejoicing with the lads who came home,
From the battles and trenches;
Where in France they did roam,
But in many people's houses,
There was a lack of the festive spirit;
As their menfolk weren't back.

For their loved ones in khaki;
Now lay side by side,
In a graveyard in France;
With their pals who had died,
And the bells did ring out,
To greet the baby Christ birth,
Whilst their hero son's lay;
In a foreign lands earth.

Their presents of sorrow,
Were all that they had,
And memories of past times,
Made them feel sad,
At Christmas let's think of that time long ago,
And what we can do to help all who feel low,
Invite them to share your meal,
And enjoy your home,
And prove to them all,
That they're not alone.

Inertia

Each morning we are told to organise our day,
But if our mood is slothful,
This often goes astray,
We feel that we must always try,
To get a good routine,
But many times we want to sit,
And survey our garden scene.

Our eyes they are too tired to read,
Our concentration nil,
We blame it on a bad night sleep,
Or prescribed sleeping pill,
What is wrong to lounge about,
Allowing our mind to wander?
But I hope it will come back to me,
When I've had my little ponder.

Those jobs that we all should do,
To tidy up the house,
But if it looks ok to me,
Then I'm not going to grouse,
My windows they need cleaning,
But I still can see outside,
To see them slightly grubby,
Does not dampen manly pride.

This feeling of inertia,
I try to cultivate,
Why bother to do anything,
That makes back and muscles ache,
My rest and recreation consist of lying flat,
At least I will be comfy,
When I have my Heart Attack!

These lines were written before the Cooling Towers and Power Station were demolished in 1985

Kearsley Power Station

The water no longer inside the towers falls,
No smoke is seen from chimneys tall,
They've shut us down; works and all,
Its what folks call redundant,
The lights still shine around the valley,
But not with power from Kearsley.
Down through the age's men have worked,
Stoking the boilers with sweat soaked shirts,
To earn their daily bread and more,
To make light shine in cottage and hall,
Five towers now stand alone and at rest,
Six chimneys provide just a Kestrel's nest.
It's got to come down the planners say,
To make way for leisure and people at play,
But towers and chimneys still stand supreme,
And look down a valley that's spry and clean,
The hum from the pylons passing close by,
Have sounded the death knell of station.
In days before station were built brick on brick,
The slag heaps of coal mines formed heap upon heap,
The mines closed down and houses were built,
Then to watch over the valley the towers did rise,
Smoke from the chimneys billowed above,
And hung over the valley where stocks and bridge stood.
It now stands alone waiting to fall,
The towers the chimneys, asbestos and all,
The workers come in and deal the death blow;
With blow torch and hammer, come in and then go,
What's left is a shell where man's great endeavour,
Built chimneys and towers that are now gone forever.

Iron Man

I've seen a paper advert to enter Iron Man,
I thought to myself, I have the skills,
And must work out a good plan,
I'll have to get in training,
For I know the course is tough,
With different kinds of disciplines,
And master them I must.

My muscles I will build up,
For I know that they'll be needed,
For speed will be essential,
As I 'm sure to be unseeded.

But as to what equipment is the best,
For my future endeavour,
I 'll have to look on't internet,
I think that's rather clever.

Its then that I was puzzled,
For it talks of bikes and shoes,
And does not mention ironing boards,
Or irons I can choose,
No mention of a counterpane,
Or blouse or pillowcase,
It seems that the iron man,
Is a different kind of race.

Loneliness

He stands there in a crowd but still feels so alone,
Surrounded by people, but inside he's on his own,
This feeling has been with him,
Since his dear wife passed on,
But still he smiles to everyone,
But his inner spark has gone,
His solitude within his home at times is like a weight,
No one to even talk to, no visitor at the gate,
The family are busy, with a life that is their own,
At times he feels abandoned;
As most of them don't phone,
He knows he is getting weary,
But at his age that is no crime,
He just cannot rush now, he's plenty of spare time,
He does a little housework, but his forte it is not,
And loneliness is something that he thinks about a lot,
The TV is no comfort regarding most of it as trash,
Though he sometimes thinks his judgement rather rash,
Memories sustain him, of his life in times gone by,
With trips he made and people met,
Brought back in his mind's eye,
Sometimes a little thoughtfulness of family and friends,
To spend a little time with him,
For on them he now depends,
To help him view the future, in not such a dismal way,
So that the lonely feelings will slowly go away.

Languidity

Today I'm feeling languid, or am I getting old?
This unenergetic feeling is normal so I'm told,
It's a symptom of the age,
When we reach our golden years,
But whoever called them golden was being so perverse,
Some people call me lazy, I prefer to say relaxed,
My attitude is somnolent, to normal daily tasks,
Friends come to visit me, not to see the dust accrued,
On the top of the sideboard;
Where it's not quite been removed,
I'm often quite lethargic, my motivation gone,
My mood is one of indolence, I'll wait till its passed on,
My apathy is palpable, but I just feel laid-back,
My bodies feeling moribund, so tasks I can't attack,
Procrastination rules my day, most things I just put off,
I'm told that I must exercise, but wine I prefer to quaff,
My day is oh so busy, my brain it's not relaxed,
Thinking of excuses not to do outstanding tasks.

The Spirit of Christmas

Egbert was not very bright,
Which meant all his chairs weren't at home,
He heard of the spirit of Christmas,
So to find it he started to roam.

He met Johnny Mac who's a Scotchman,
"It's whisky you're needing my lad,
In Scotland that's spirit of Christmas,
So have a wee dram,
You'll find it tastes none too bad,"
Egbert he downed the tot in a second,
He'd never supped whisky before,
It felt like a fire in his belly,
As he headed for hotel's front door.

That can't be the spirit of Christmas,
He thought as his legs felt peculiar and queer,
So he asked a mate Colin for guidance,
And his answer was "let's have a beer,"
Is that the spirit of Christmas?
"Sure is" was Colin's reply,
"It cultivates friendship and merriment,
Like you had when you were a boy."

Edgar downed a couple of swift pints,
But he did not feel right in his head,
That can't be the spirit of Christmas he thought,
I must get home to my bed,
I've got to find the spirit of Christmas,
They say that it's always about.

But just as he got to the street where he lived,
His neighbour gave him a shout,
"Have some Mulled wine with me my dear friend,
It tastes so much better than tea,"
Poor Edgar not wishing to hurt the chap's feelings,
Felt he just had to agree,
So into his house he tottered,
Head swimming, and feet all askew,
He woke up the following morning,
Feeling queasy and head thumping too.

His friend had put him on his sofa,
And asked how he felt this fine morn,
So he found the true spirit of Christmas,
On a couch the day Christ was born.

Mum's Washday

Washday always Monday,
In times now long since passed,
I watched my mum fill up the tub,
Turn on the heating gas,
The whites they bubbled nicely,
So clean and bright they'd shine,
And the addition of a "Dolly Blue",
Would make them look real fine.

With washing tongues she'd lift the sheets,
Into a waiting Dolly Tub,
Then move the posser up and down,
So all sheets had a rub,
Mum had the perfect movement,
As she used the metal rubbing board,
With masses of Fairy soap,
So cleanness was assured.

Fastened to the table above the Dolly Tub,
Was a hand powered Acme wringer,
For her use after the scrub,
She would slowly turn the handle,
And squeeze the water out,
It helped the sheets to dry out,
Of that there was no doubt.

On sunny days out they would go,
To dry in the noonday sun,
But on rainy days they dried inside,
Which never was such fun,
The air was damp and steamy,
And condensation filled the room,

Sheets hung from racks in the ceiling,
Which contributed to the gloom.

The toil of the washday,
Was part of our mother's daily grind,
Now automatics and spin driers,
Give folks much more leisure time.

Lines written after the terrorist bomb attack at the Ariana Grande Concert at Manchester Arena on 22 May 2017.

My Manchester

Manchester's hurting its people are sad,
For the slaughter they witnessed,
Was more than just bad,
A mindless act by a terrorist fiend,
Caused the death of the innocents,
Where joy had just been,
Our city is famous for its friendly persona,
Its caring and sharing, its music and humour,
All came together to help the injured and strangers,
With compassion and kindness midst terrorist dangers,
This city will never be submissive and cowed,
Mancunians are strong, open hearted and proud.

Lines written after the terrorist attacks in London 2017.

The North and the South

We came together the north and the south,
No terrorist will divide us were British and proud,
Patriotic, unflinching midst terrorist threat,
Caused by minds twisted with hatred,
We've not fathomed yet,
The north and the south of this country of ours,
Were battered and shocked as the carnage unfolded,
We feel for the, injured, the frightened, the slain,
Purportedly committed, in Allah's name,
This cannot be true as most Muslims declaim,
The actions of a few, sully their good name,
A nation divided is no nation at all,
No threats should divide us, as actions appal,
Manchester, London, great cities united,
In love with our city's the Zealots have blighted.

The Robin

When walking in our local park,
A robin I espied,
Sitting there as bold as brass,
It looked me in the eye,
It seemed to say, "now watch your step,
You're in my patch you know,
There's only food enough for me,
So you had better go,"
T'was on a branch so near to me,
With feathers puffed and proud,
His red breast gleaming in the sun,
His stance upright not cowed,
The moment it was magical,
With man and bird in tune,
The meeting happening in a park,
On a sunny afternoon,
In my mind's eye I still can see,
That Robin sentinel,
Protecting what he thought was his,
From the likes of me.

The Spider

It found a nice dark corner,
To spin its lethal trap,
Each silken strand as fine as hair,
Its prey to then entrap,
Built with such care and patience,
Its beauty you behold,
When winter frosts encase it;
It shines as if 'twere gold,
The spider waits to see,
What fruits his labour will provide,
And what delicious morsel,
Down his gullet it will glide,
It spins it's webs in summertime,
And when the winter winds do blow,
It drapes its threads in buildings,
And even great chateau,
In houses they cause trauma,
To the house-proud resident,
Who seek out every spider's web,
On eradication their hell bent,
But those of us who see beauty,
In all of nature's creatures,
Just watch the humble spider,
And admire its silken features.

The Room

Your room is warm and comforting,
Where memories abound,
You sit in contemplation,
With silence all around,
You look towards that empty chair,
Where the one you miss, did sit,
And imagine her sitting there,
Safe home whilst she did knit.

But cruelly taken, far too early,
And you left on your own,
You have only memories,
As you sit at home alone,
You long to share a book you read,
Or just discuss the plot,
But the empty chair is all you see,
So your wishes come to naught.

Loneliness is something,
That one feels as you grow old,
Your partner gone, your friends deceased,
But still you soldier on,
The daily routine carries on,
You talk to all you meet,
But when the front door closes,
There's no one there to greet.

In summer there's the garden for you to cultivate,
But wintertime means long dark nights,
A time most do hate,
Your limbs no longer supple,
Your joints they creak and groan,

The aches and pains of old age,
Means you suffer on your own.

But don't despair you still have time,
To occupy your mind,
To do the morning crossword,
And puzzles that you find,
Don't stagnate watching TV,
And mindless daytime soaps,
Your body may be shattered,
But your minds still keen one hopes!

The Yule Log

The yule log burns and flickers,
In the blazing hearth,
Lighting up the darkness,
With the light it does impart,
Brought in from the forest,
To last till the New Year.

It signifies the season,
At the ending of the year,
No matter what the weather in the outside air,
The yule logs cheerful flicker warms hearts,
And dispels all care,
So gather round the fireside,
With those you hold most dear,
And remember all the happy times,
You had throughout the year.

Thoughts on a farewell

Yesterday we said goodbye and celebrated,
The life of one so loved,
And people gathered from afar,
To say a sad farewell,
But also memories surrounded us,
Of a life we knew so well,
Whilst images of happy times,
Within our minds did dwell,
At times like this we realise,
That our loved ones do not die,
Though seen no more,
Their spirit sings to us a lullaby,
Our sadness cannot take away,
The joy that did abound,
When we heard her merry laughter,
And heard her voice's sound,
She would not wish for sadness,
To dominate our days,
But live a life to honour her,
To the ending of our days.

Washing Mishap

My friend she got her smalls out,
To do the weekly wash,
Loaded washer carefully,
With soap that goes splish, splosh,
Closed the door heard the click,
That told her all was well,
Pushed the starting button,
Then came the big bombshell,
The lights they flashed,
No hum was heard,
The darn thing would not go,
Despite her ministrations,
'Twas stopped which was a blow,
It seemed her motherboard was bent,
The spindle would not turn,
Her drum it would not revolve,
Which caused her great concern,
So now my friend must splash some cash,
To mend her poorly washer,
Or else get the scrubbing board,
The mangle and the posser.

Winter Days

Snow and sleet and driving rain,
Winter gales do blow again,
Dark clouds drifting in the sky,
Are heralds to bad weathers cry,
People muffled in the street,
Boots and gloves on hands and feet,
Coats of leather, coats of down,
Wrapped up warm for a trip to town,
Birds all cluster in the trees,
Snuggled up to beat the freeze,
Cloudless sky, winter frost,
Hedgerows glisten, birdsong lost,
Barn owls hunting in the dusk,
Finding food is a night time must,
Farmyard foxes, hungry deer,
Scavenge round for winter cheer,
Bleak and desolate moorland stretches,
Hidden by snow the moss and vetches,
Essential food for grouse and deer,
They seek in the snow when winters here,
Upland sheep round stone walls cluster,
Shelter from the strong winds bluster,
Trees skeletal, devoid of leaves,
Swaying in the cold winds breeze,
All these elements do combine,
To make this country's winter time.

Witches Party

At Halloween a party' held,
At the castle on the hill,
The invites go to witches,
From as far away a Rhyl!!
Best robes on and pointy hats,
With broomsticks polished too,
To feast on a tasty stew,
From cauldron coloured blue,
Eye of newt and toe of frog,
A rotten fish or two,
A viper's tongue and hedgehogs spine's,
Go in that witch's stew,
The spells they cast are awesome,
And thunder it does roar,
With lightening flash they terrify,
Any people that go near,
The skeletons they dance a jig,
To the beat of a ghoulish band,
Whilst the witches tap their broomsticks,
On any tombstone that's to hand,
The Vampires from the castle,
Serve cups of wine that's red,
Though where that wine has come,
From fills me with such dread,
At daybreak they all vanish,
From that spooky castle wall,
But we are certain that they'll be back,
For the Christmas Witches Ball.

I have a problem in my house, which I am sure afflicts many homes and at times it drives me nuts!!

My walking mats.

I have a certain problem,
Which blights my night time hours,
My house is in possession of a thing,
Playing games within my bower,
Each night I align my mats and rungs,
In doorways and by beds,
They look so neat and ordered,
And are right just where I tread,
But this silent poltergeist like thing,
Positions mats anew,
For on going to the loo each morn,
My mats are now askew,
It seems it does not like my placing mats all straight,
My mats have moved, I know now why,
I hate them in this state,
I've thought to bring a warlock in,
For incantations and cast spells,
But he says that Wilton and Axminister,
Are things he can't dispel,
I've tried the local vicar, but his look just says I'm daft,
And dismisses my pleas with an enigmatic laugh,
So I have now to put up with mats,
That walk about each night,
And my doctor says that I must change,
This ritual of my plight,
OCD rules my days,
But at night time I am scuppered,
I will just have to wait,
Until a cure has been discovered.

Nativity

Parents they all gathered to see the nativity play,
The school had worked so hard,
To make sure 'twas right today,
But the little junior players,
Were not sure of all their lines,
Poor Mary had the hiccups,
And Joseph's laughter was unkind.

The angels they danced on stage,
But then disaster struck,
The fluffy wings upon their backs, fell off,
As glue became unstuck,
Poor little angel Gabriel,
Began to howl and weep,
Which startled all the little tots,
Who were all dressed up as sheep.

The inn keeper he took charge,
And yelled "you two had better scarper,
Mi rooms are full you can see,
Your room booking should have been sharper,
Joseph then got shirty,
"Mi donkey he is shattered,
And Mary's not much better,
We'll sleep in yonder stable,
Though the straw will mess her sweater."

Now William was the Bethlehem star,
And held his stick up high,
But the heat on stage and all the din,
Made him start to cry,
The teacher rushed to comfort him,

But tripped upon the stage,
And ended up upon the crib,
Where baby Jesus laid.

The three wise men viewed the scene,
And thought what should we do?
But then one said to Joseph,
"I've some Frankenstein for you,"
The parents started laughing,
The best line in the show,
But the crying chaos on the stage,
Dealt it a fatal blow.

We all look forward to next year,
For none of us can tell,
What mishap will then befall,
The Nativity Clientele.

On Camera

George Orwell was the man,
Who said that Big Brother watches all,
But it seems to me that nowadays,
It's the myriad cameras that appal,
You cannot walk down any street,
Without their silent gaze,
As someone sits and watches you,
When in shopping your engaged,
But get into your motor car,
And ride the nation's bye ways,
But woe betide you if you speed,
They'll catch you on the highways,
No matter where you go these days,
You feature in their lenses,
You cannot hide in crowds no more,
It's the intrusion that incenses,
Your free to roam our country,
But on your own you're not,
For high above you in the sky,
A drone is what you spot,
For now, the countries ringed with cameras,
That orbit us in space,
From miles above they see us,
And take pictures of your face,
Even at home you're not secure,
As tv's tech we now allow,
It's the curse of modern living,
Big Brothers here and now.

Parliamentary Politics.

I used to think that politics,
Was demure and so refined,
With arguments persuasive,
And politely well defined,
That gentlemanly conduct was the norm,
Or so I'm told,
And parliament embodied,
All the best ideals we hold,
But lately I'm afraid,
That my vision has been shattered,
With hackles raised its members leave,
Its reputation battered,
The dispatch box marks a battleground,
Between the warring sides,
And venom, spite and vitriol,
Emphasise what does divide,
When seen on television,
They look like fighting cats,
With both side hurling insults,
Being unlike good democrats,
The public are all sick of the antics,
Of this childish baying mob,
And would love to see a parliament,
That politely does its job,
Where differences are aired in an educated way,
And discussion is the cornerstone of democracy today.

Post Festive Thoughts

The Christmas splurge is over,
Boxing Day's been boxed,
The presents have been played with,
And sweets, the kids have scoffed the lot,
The relatives have all gone home,
Empty bottles in the bin,
And only New Year to endure,
When some diets will begin,
We look at our waistlines,
And vow to get them slimmer,
But then we gorge on turkey,
At a festive New Year dinner,
Our heads are still a thumping,
Our livers gone on strike,
We feel a kind of queasiness,
From this festive drink laden hike,
We look towards the coming year,
To begin our new routine,
But in our hearts, we all know,
It's another festive dream.

Potholes.

There is a creeping plague,
Afflicting this fair land,
At first you hardly notice it,
Just hear the odd loud bang,
But as you drive upon the road,
You notice bigger things,
It seems your exhaust has developed a funny sort of ring,
Your car it starts to rattle,
As you navigate the street,
Your body it starts bouncing,
As you sit upon your seat,
This creeping menace, slowly permeates your brain,
Your car it bucks and clatters,
As though you're on a train,
The road is like a switchback,
Its worse when it is wet,
For the council workforce has no time to fill them yet.
The creeping pothole phantom is resident in this land,
And council's say the money to repair them,
At presents not to hand,
Some say the local garages have paid the beast to come,
So they can make a fortune,
From the damage it has done,
Exhausts they are a rattling,
And springs they creak and groan,
And mechanics rub their hands with glee,
At the money they take home,
Please have a whip-round,
To solve this deadly plague,
So we can drive in safety,
And not suffer from road- rage.

Rambling

When I was a young lad,
A rambling I did go,
Out into the countryside,
Which made my face to glow,
But as the waistline did expand,
And my hair was tinged with grey,
I'm afraid the moorland tramping,
Did not make my day.

I'd lounge about on the couch,
Watch Countryfile on the telly,
So inches did accumulate,
Around my expanding belly,
The doctor who examined me,
Said I had become a sloth,
And exercise was the thing,
That I lacked the most.

So filled with mortification,
At my far from lithe condition,
To the Hiking shop I went to buy,
A kit for my expedition,
First the boots, how they had changed,
No clinkers or tricouni's,
Cleated soles with soft suede tops,
And socks all soft and foamy.

My army Kagoule now replaced,
With a trendy yellow jacket,
The salesman said it was breathable,
But it'll cost me quite a packet,
No jeans on the hillside,

Its moleskin that's in fashion,
And maps and compass are a must,
Their prices made me ashen.
You'll have to buy a sat nav,
As well as mobile phone,
Just in case you get lost,
In rough country as you roam.

We've a nice line in rucksacks,
The salesman said to me,
Only one to two hundred pounds,
A bargain as you'll see,
Survival gear was next on't list,
First aid and Bivi bag,
And walking poles will help you,
As your old and tend to lag.

I stood there pale and ashen,
Retro-sternal was my pain,
The prices that were quoted,
Caused me shock and great disdain,
To Hospital with Heart Attack,
In shock and feeling battered,
But my money was still in my bank,
And that was what really mattered,
I'm now too frail to roam the hills,
And the doc told me to rest,
So tramping in the countryside,
Still leaves me unimpressed.

Mum, Dad and Grandad planned a secret trip in August 2018.

The Trip

The trip was planned in secret,
As the kids were not to know,
For the Morgan's nosy parkers,
Are always on the go,
One of them is an expert at listening,
To parents making plans,
He just did not contemplate,
This trip to far off lands.

Tickets they were ordered,
And rooms booked on the sly,
And Mum and Dad did not talk,
Within the hearing of their spy,
For when the day came,
To pack the car and go,
Our two intrepid travellers,
Where still not in the know.

They went and picked up Grandad,
And were very mystified,
When instead of going for a walk,
He got into the car and sat inside,
We sped along the motorway,
The questions they came fast,
But not a clue as to where we were,
Or how long the trip would last.

A service station came in view,
We decamped and had a brew,

But Alfie had of course to go,
And inspect the nearest loo!
The drive it lasted hours,
And dad was hot and tired,
The kids they were mystified,
The trip homes taking hours,
We drove into a Motel,
And said we'd stay the night,
And we were very thankful,
That no leaflets were in sight.

Next morning on the TV,
They found that London was not far,
But going there they were not,
As they got into the car,
Their shock it was compounded,
When through the gates they sped,
To Magic Harry Potter Land,
And its massive film lot spread,
The look on their faces,
Wreathed in smiles and wonderment,
Show just how much our secret trip,
To them was Heaven-sent.

I was a member of the Bolton Mountain Rescue Team for 20 plus years and wrote this poem, after attending the 50th Celebration Dinner of the team.

Bolton Mountain Rescue
50th Anniversary

It is 50 years since the team began,
All hardy souls to a man,
Who thought that people hurt,
On moors and mountain peaks,
Deserved help and expertise,
Their pain and anguish to appease,
All people gathered to celebrate,
Past achievements, to meet old friends,
And how the years have ringed the changes,
As we view forgotten faces,
But gathered there, that easy fellowship still remains,
As they relived those heady days,
Of Mountain Rescues early days,
Of cash strapped team, and clapped out vans,
Still keen to help the stricken man,
Alone and lost on mountain side,
So with good humour and resolve,
Set out to locate and bring home safe,
That climber, hiker, from the hills,
That give such pleasure, but sometimes kill,
The team has prospered from those days,
But the principle still remains,
To be there throughout the year,
In rain and snow or winter chill,
Through training, knowledge, and skill,
When duty calls they'll be there still.

The Ache Inside.

Its three years now since I watched her pass away,
I still can visualise the scene,
The change in sound, then the last long sigh,
The numbness that I felt then, has never left,
But life with its pattern still carries on,
Like flotsam in the sea: it propels us forward,
Time does not stop: life for us goes on,
It does nothing to ease the ache one feels,
But merely dulls it for a time,
Then on looking at an object or image,
We can recreate that time: when we were two not one,
In all its vivid detail: the ache returns then fades,
Returning to that place within our being,
Until memories cause it to return.

The Blackbird

Each morning high atop the elm,
The blackbird greets the sun,
And from its lofty perch on high,
Its morning songs begun,
It matters not if rain doth fall,
Or frost coats twig and branch,
Its lilting melody and trills,
Tells morning-tide has come,
It tells the flowers to open,
And other birds to sing,
So that the dawn time chorus,
Blends in with howling wind,
It sings through spring and summer,
Tis music to the ear,
And fills our hearts with joyous song,
All seasons of the year,
If you whistle to the blackbird,
A reply you'll quickly hear,
Just to say good day to you,
And fill you with good cheer.

The Church

You open the door it creaks at your touch,
Slip into the building and silence surrounds,
The wind through the rafters plays its own tune,
Coloured light from the windows,
Fill the space in this room,
A feeling of peace enters your soul,
It can't be explained, but this feeing enfolds,
The columns, woodwork, statues and cross,
Help to console when you feel at a loss,
So many have come to this place over time,
Rituals are done, which at times are sublime,
But when cares and sadness burden your mind,
You can escape here, and stay for some time,
Reflect on the problems that life's asked you to bear,
And hope that it gives you, some relief from despair,
Its been a sanctuary since times now long past,
It's a symbol of caring that we hope will last.

Moonbeams

The moonlight enters every room,
In the village by the shore,
Each house is bathed in golden light,
The moon lights up each door.

And every house is occupied,
Some folks are sound asleep,
Whilst others tread the carpets,
Night time vigils they do keep.

Perhaps some fisherman's true love,
Anguished for her beau,
Upon the seas at midnight,
Working in the lamplights glow.

In one house a baby cry's,
For sustenance this night,
Whilst down the street a woman weeps,
I know not what her plight.

A policeman on his night patrol,
Slowly plods his beat,
A dark and lonely figure,
As he wanders down the street.

The student crouched in study,
Cramming for next day's exam,
He should have started days ago,
But said, he did not give a damn.

The moonbeams through the windows,
Causes shadows in each room,

And imagination plays tricks,
Within its shaded corners gloom.

And people's hearts beat faster,
As they misinterpret what they see,
And terrify us mortals,
The likes of you and me.

An all-pervading silence,
Disturbed by ticking clock,
Leaves us straining to hear untoward sounds,
And hoping that they stop.

The dawn it slowly creeps its way,
To light the daytime sky,
Causing all the moonbeams to disappear and fly.

More Author's From Violet Circle Publishing

Mike Beale.
Crumble's Adventures.   *Children's Fiction.*

Discover the wonderful world of Crumble, the little dog with a nose for friends and adventure. This delightful story is an ideal read for young children making their way into advanced reading, and also a wonderful story for mum and dad to read at bedtime.

Robin John Morgan.
Heirs to the Kingdom.   *Fantasy Adventure Series.*

A fast paced and action packed adventure set in the future after the world is devastated by a deadly virus bringing about the end of modern life as we know it. Join a young boy who has an unnatural talent with a long bow, as he leads a group of his woodland dwelling friends against the might of the powerful Mason Knox. This fantasy adventure takes threads of the past and weaves them into a modern, captivating, and thought provoking tale of the struggle of the woodland people, as they fight to preserve their life at peace within nature.

Ted Morgan.
Wordsmith's Wanderings.   *Poetry And Rhymes.*

Wordsmith's Wandering is a simple delight to read. Based on the life and observations of the author this reflective and at time very humours collection of poems and rhymes, reflect the 76 years of a man who has served in national service and the health system, whilst also working as a member of the mountain rescue team.

Colin Smith.
Heaven Knows I'm Miserable Now.   *Stage Play*

Is death really the end? Andy Reardon is about to find out, and he's beginning to wish it was. When Andy discovers his number is up, he finds the afterlife is not exactly fluffy clouds, harps, and Saint Peter.
What will Andy do about his dead wives?
He has three of them, all chomping at the bit to see Andy again but none of them are quite how Andy remembers. With Jesus Christ and Adolph Hitler dishing out advice, Andy might make the right decision, and be happy for all eternity. This black comedy takes Andy on the trip of a death time, and leaves him to make choices he'd never dream he would ever have to make.

Find out more about our authors, and their books at
www.violetcirclepublishing.co.uk

Violet Circle Publishing, Manchester, UK

www.ingramcontent.com/pod-product-compliance
Lightning Source LLC
Chambersburg PA
CBHW070044230426
43661CB00005B/751